Maps and Globes

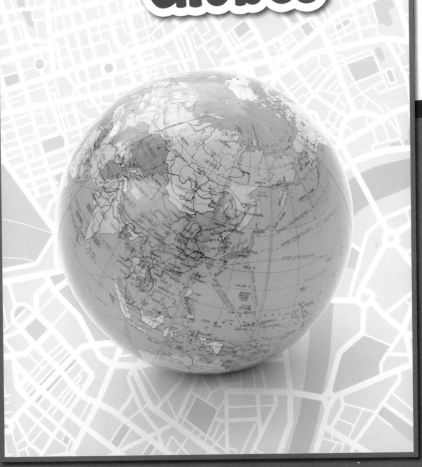

Dona Herweck Rice

Consultants

Mabel Huddleston
Tustin Unified School District

Publishing Credits

Rachelle Cracchiolo, M.S.Ed., *Publisher* Conni Medina, M.A.Ed., *Managing Editor* Emily R. Smith, M.A.Ed., *Series Developer*
June Kikuchi, *Content Director*
Susan Daddis, M.A.Ed., *Editor*
Courtney Roberson, *Senior Graphic Designer*

Image Credits: p.20 Samantha Kenney; all other images iStock and/or Shutterstock.

Library of Congress Cataloging-in-Publication Data

Names: Rice, Dona, author.
Title: Maps and globes / Dona Herweck Rice.
Description: Huntington Beach, CA : Teacher Created Materials, [2018] | Includes index. | Audience: Grades: K to Grade 3.
Identifiers: LCCN 2017053265 (print) | LCCN 2018001748 (ebook) | ISBN 9781425825577 | ISBN 9781425825157 (paperback)
Subjects: LCSH: Maps--Juvenile literature. | Globes--Juvenile literature.
Classification: LCC GA105.6 (ebook) | LCC GA105.6 .R53 2018 (print) | DDC 912--dc23
LC record available at https://lccn.loc.gov/2017053265

Teacher Created Materials
5301 Oceanus Drive
Huntington Beach, CA 92649-1030
www.tcmpub.com
ISBN 978-1-4258-2515-7

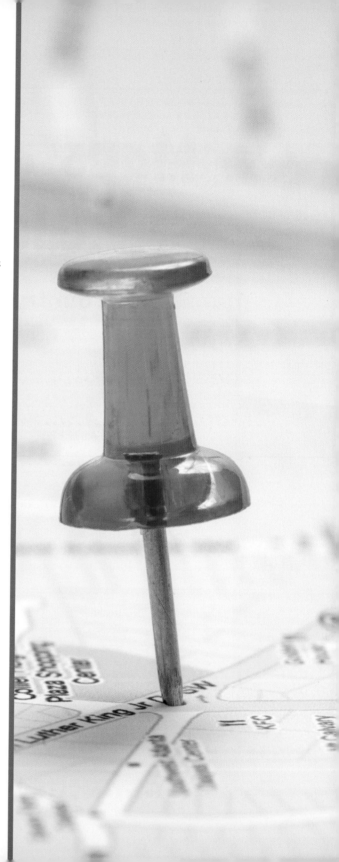

Table of Contents

Fairburn Rd SW

The World in Your Hands

Be an **explorer**! Anyone can explore with a map in hand. Maps and globes show where you are going and where you have been. If you can read a map, the world is in your hands!

globe

On the Map

America was first used on a map in 1507. That map still exists. It is worth a lot of money!

world map

Your Neighborhood

The world is a big place, and your **neighborhood** is one small part of it. It is where you live. It is the place you know best. You know your street. A park or a playground may also be in your neighborhood.

This picture shows Los Angeles.

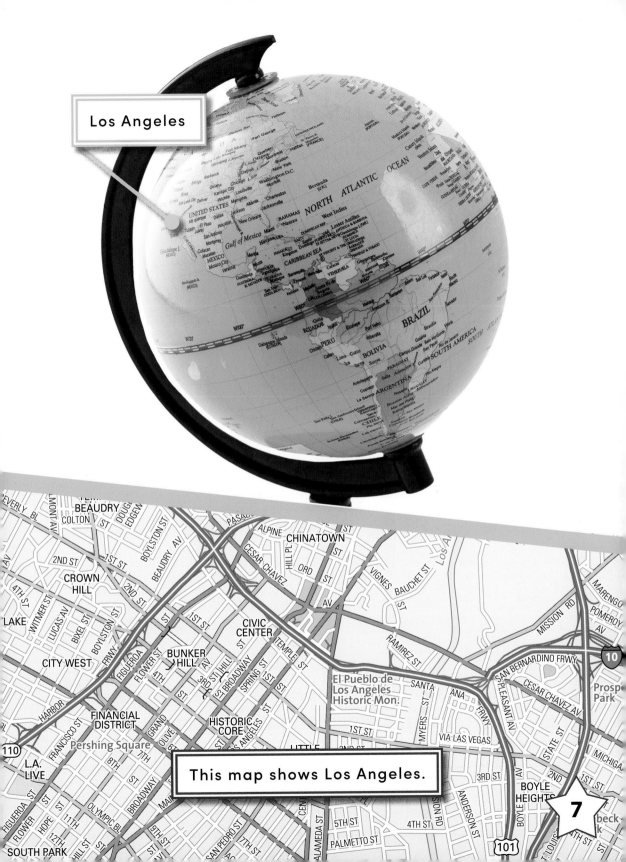

Los Angeles

This map shows Los Angeles.

Your neighborhood is in your community. Stores and your school may be there as well. A fire station may be nearby. There may be a post office, too. A map can help you find these places.

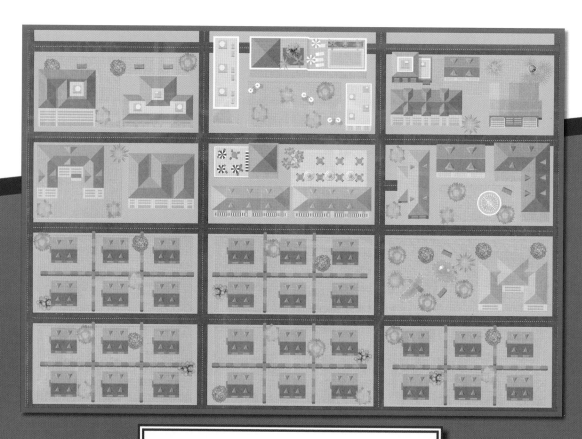

This map shows a neighborhood.

Which Way?

Maps help you find your way. They tell you which direction to go. The four main directions are north, south, east, and west.

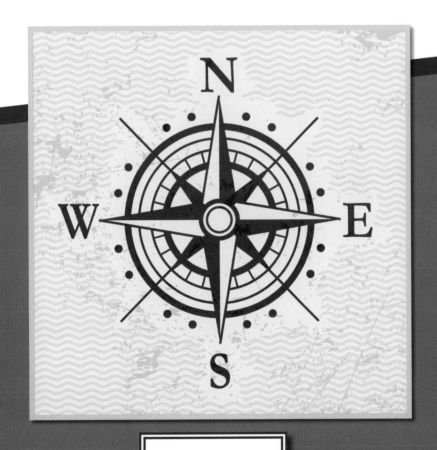

compass rose

A map shows where to find places in your community. It shows how to drive or walk to each place. Learn to read a map to plan your **route**. There may be more than one route to a place you want to go. The map will show you.

This map shows two routes from this house to the library.

Your State, Country, and the World

Your community is one of many in your state. All the cities and towns are shown on a state map. A state map also shows rivers and lakes. It shows roads and highways.

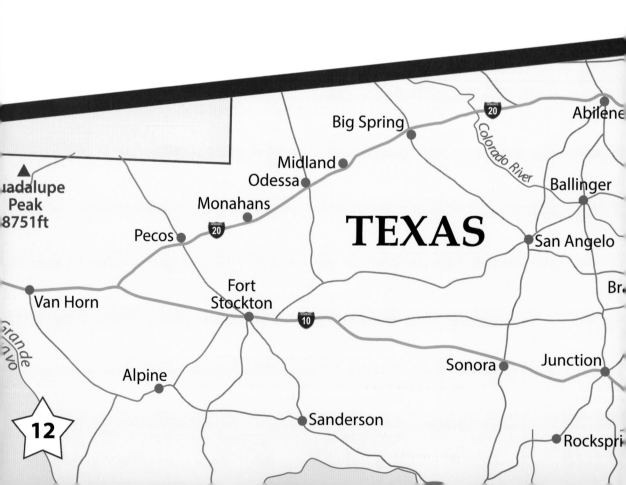

What Does It Mean?

Maps use symbols and colors to explain things. Stars are used to show state capitals. Lakes and rivers are blue. Mountains are often brown.

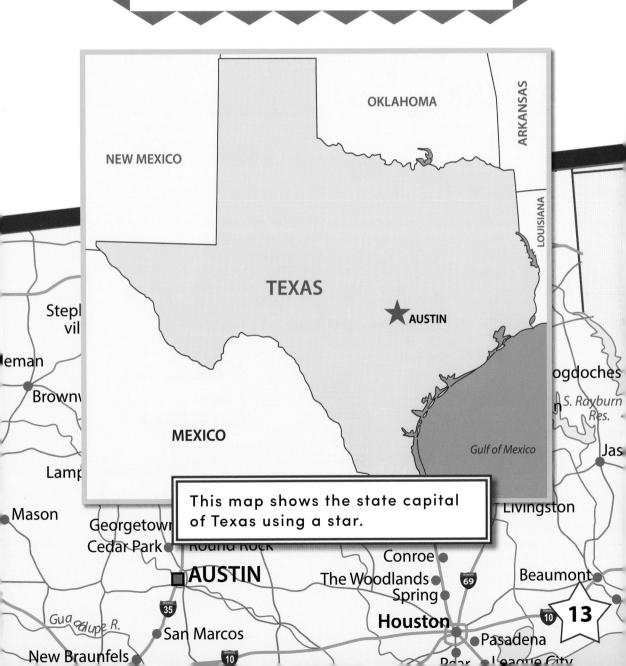

This map shows the state capital of Texas using a star.

13

Your state is one of many in the United States of America, which is a country. Maps of your country show each state. They mark **borders**. They show big cities. Mountains are on maps. Other land **features**, such as lakes, are shown on some maps, too.

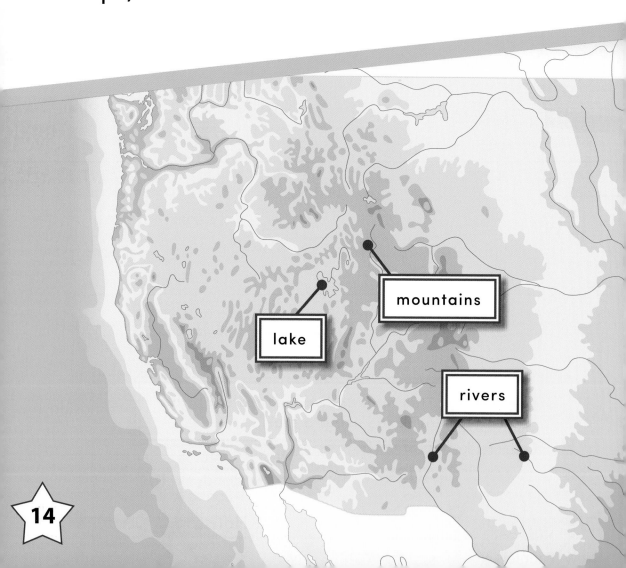

mountains

lake

rivers

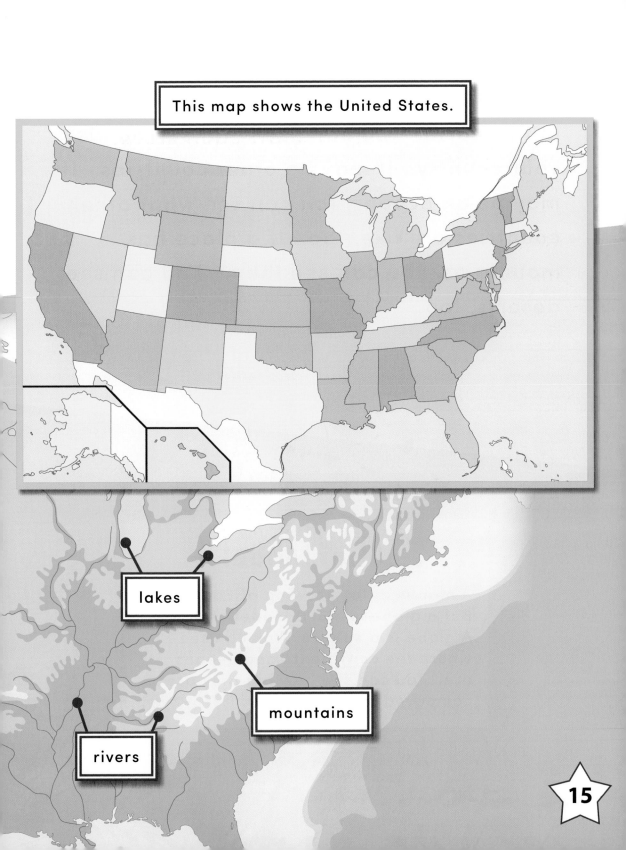

This map shows the United States.

lakes

mountains

rivers

15

Each country can also be found on a globe. A globe shows where a country is in the world. You can see what surrounds your country. It may be other countries. It may be an ocean. You can see what other countries are like, too. If a place has mountains, you can see them. You can see deserts, too.

Mini Model

A map is a flat drawing of Earth. But a globe is a 3-D model of it. A globe is a **sphere**. You can see where the **continents** and oceans are. You can see how big they are compared to one another.

A globe shows the shape of Earth.

See the World!

With a map and a globe, you can explore new places. They show you where to go. They show you what to expect once you get there.

With a map in hand, you are ready to see the world!

Did You Know?

Maps can also help you know what it is like to live in a place. Some maps even tell you the weather!

Map It!

Make a map of a room in your house or school. Draw the map as though you are looking down on the room. Show the walls, windows, and doors.

Give your finished map to a friend. Can your friend guess what the map shows?

Glossary

borders—the outer lines that separate a country or state

continents—large pieces of land on Earth

explorer—a person who travels and studies places

features—distinct or special areas

neighborhood—the area right around where a person lives

route—path to get you somewhere

sphere—a solid, round 3-D shape

Index

Your Turn!

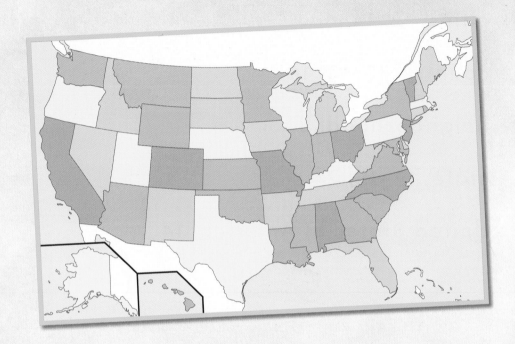

Name My State

Find your state on the map. Look at the states around it. Think of three clues about where your state is. Share your clues with a friend. See if he or she can name your state.